SNOWMOBILE RACERS

Bob Woods

Enslow Publishers, Inc.
40 Industrial Road
Box 398
Berkeley Heights, NJ 07922
USA

http://www.enslow.com

Library of Congress Cataloging-in-Publication Data
Woods, Bob.
  Snowmobile racers / Bob Woods.
    p. cm. — (Kid racers)
  Includes bibliographical references and index.
  Summary: "High interest book for reluctant readers containing action packed
photos and stories of the hottest snowmobiles and races for kids, discussing which
snowmobiles qualify, how they are built and raced, who the best drivers are, what to
look for in a snowmobile, safety, good sportsmanship, and how racing activities can be
a good part of family life"—Provided by publisher.
  ISBN 978-0-7660-3487-7
  1. Snowmobile racing—Juvenile literature. I. Title.
  GV856.8.W66 2010
  796.94—dc22
                        2009020784

ISBN 978-0-7660-3756-4 (paperback)

Printed in the United States of America

102009 Lake Book Manufacturing, Inc., Melrose Park, IL

10 9 8 7 6 5 4 3 2 1

To Our Readers:
We have done our best to make sure all Internet addresses in this book were active
and appropriate when we went to press. However, the author and the publisher have
no control over and assume no liability for the material available on those Internet
sites or on other Web sites they may link to. Any comments or suggestions can be sent
by e-mail to comments@enslow.com or to the address on the back cover.
    Any stunts shown in this book have been performed by experienced riders and
should not be attempted by beginners.

♻ Enslow Publishers, Inc., is committed to printing our books on recycled paper.
The paper in every book contains 10% to 30% post-consumer waste (PCW). The cover
board on the outside of each book contains 100% PCW. Our goal is to do our part to
help young people and the environment too!

Adviser: *Doug Rust, director of events, International Series of Champions*

Cover Photo Credit: J&L Photography
Interior Photo Credits: Corbis/Underwood & Underwood, p. 8; Corbis/Bo Bridges,
p. 13; Corbis/Layne Kennedy, p. 24; Courtesy of Dallas Ostrom, pp. 38, 39 (top);
Getty Images, p. 6; Getty Images/Doug Pensinger, p. 36; Getty Images/Steve Mason,
p. 40; iStockphoto.com/monroejournal, p. 5; iStockphoto.com/LifeJourneys, p. 28;
iStockphoto.com/Dan Driedger, p. 29; iStockphoto.com/Laila Roberg, pp. 38–39;
iStockphoto.com/Tony Tremblay, p. 41; J&L Photography, pp. 1, 4, 9, 10, 14, 15, 16, 20,
22, 23, 26, 27, 30, 31, 32, 33, 34, 35, 37, 42, 43; Courtesy of Snowmobile Hall of Fame,
11 (bottom); Courtesy of Yamaha Motor Corporation USA, pp. 11 (top), 18–19, 19 (top),
21, 39 (bottom).

Contents

1 RACE DAY! 4

2 THE GREATEST SHOW ON SNOW 6

3 SNOWMOBILE HISTORY: THE HARD, COLD FACTS . . 8

4 STAR MANUFACTURERS 10

5 SO YOU WANT TO BE A SLED HEAD? 12

6 SHOPPING FOR SLEDS 14

7 MEET THE MACHINES 16

8 BODY BASICS 18

9 UNDER THE HOOD 20

10 FOLLOW THE TRACKS 22

11 SLED SAFETY 24

12 LOOKING GOOD, STAYING WARM . . . 26

13 RIDER BEWARE! 28

14 READY . . . SET . . . GO! 30

15 X GAMES MARK THE SPOT 32

16 SLED HEADS VS. GRAVITY 34

17 STAR RIDERS 36

18 SLICK MY SLED 38

19 THE FAMILY THAT SLEDS TOGETHER 40

20 HAPPY HAY DAYS 42

GLOSSARY 44

FURTHER READING 46

INDEX 48

Snowmobiling is a popular activity for the whole family, including kids of all ages.

RACE DAY!

The moment you wake up, you jump out of bed and run to the window. "Yippee," you cheer. "It's snowing!" You quickly pull on your thermal underwear, turtleneck sweater, and snowsuit. "I'll be right there," you holler to your mom. Breakfast is ready.

"Slow down!" your dad says as you gobble up a stack of pancakes, bacon, and orange juice.

"I don't want to be late for the race, Dad. It starts at 10, and we have to be at the course at 9:30. And look at all that snow outside!"

"Don't worry," answers your dad. "I loaded your snowmobile onto the trailer last night. I already shoveled the driveway, and the roads are plowed. We'll be there in plenty of time."

You kiss your mom and shout goodbye to your little sister. "Bring home another trophy!" she yells back.

"No problem," you exclaim.

Who are you? You are a snowmobile racer.

Let It Snow, Let It Snow, Let It Snow

These are the ten snowiest U.S. states (in alphabetical order):

A snowmobiler near Mt. McKinley in Alaska

❄ Alaska
❄ California
❄ Colorado
❄ Idaho
❄ Montana
❄ New York
❄ Oregon
❄ Utah
❄ Washington
❄ Wyoming

THE GREATEST SHOW ON SNOW

Nearly 1.6 million Americans own snowmobiles. Every winter, dads, moms, teenagers, and even little kids climb aboard their hot machines for some cold-weather fun. Some go for casual rides on groomed trails across snow-covered fields. Others dare to cut their own trails on mountainsides. When lakes freeze solid, you'll spot snowmobilers zipping along the thick ice. Snowmobiling is a social activity—there are hundreds of snowmobile clubs in snowy states.

Snocross and Other Sports

Some snowmobile racers compete in the action-packed sport of snocross. Snocross is similar

A family of snowmobilers fuels up for a ride in Yellowstone National Park.

to motocross racing on BMX bicycles and motorcycles, except it's on snow instead of dirt. In snocross, sled heads (a nickname for snowmobilers) battle each other on a course with tight turns, banked corners, steep jumps, and tricky obstacles.

Other types of snowmobile racing are ice ovals, hillcross, hillclimb, drags, cross-country, and freestyle. There are even warm-weather drag races on grass, pavement, and water!

Racing in Packs

Most amateur race events have separate groups for adults, teenagers, and younger kids. Adult professionals and semipros compete for trophies, cash prizes, and annual championships.

Where the Snowmobiles Roam

These are the ten U.S. states with the most snowmobiles (as of 2008):

Michigan (350,217 officially registered)

Minnesota (253,730)

New York (128,233)

New Hampshire (60,000)

Alaska (55,246)

Idaho (52,212)

Pennsylvania (42,118)

Illinois (38,724)

Montana (39,531)

Colorado (33,550)

Russian officers drive an early snowmobile through the city of Petrograd in the early 1900s.

SNOWMOBILE HISTORY: THE HARD, COLD FACTS

Today's high-tech snowmobiles are far different from the first motorized vehicles on skis. The aerosan was invented in Russia in the early 1900s. It was a boxy vehicle powered by a propeller. People used it to deliver mail and supplies to frozen, out-of-the-way places.

Right on Track

It was also a Russian—Adolphe Kégresse—who invented the first beltlike metal track. He put skis under the wheels of cars and trucks, and the metal track propelled them over snow.

Time for Some Fun

In the late 1930s, a Canadian man named Joseph-Armand Bombardier began tinkering with large tracked vehicles used for work and military purposes. In 1959, he introduced a smaller, "personal" version with a lighter engine. He called it the Ski-Doo. This vehicle launched the brand-new sport of snowmobiling.

Monkey See, Monkey Ski-Doo

After the first Ski-Doo appeared in 1959, dozens of manufacturers started making copycat sleds. From 1970 to 1973, almost 2 million snowmobiles were sold. However, most of those companies soon went out of business. Today there are just four major snowmobile brands: Arctic Cat, Polaris, Ski-Doo, and Yamaha.

This 1962 Ski-Doo snowmobile is on display at the Eagle River Derby Museum in Wisconsin.

STAR MANUFACTURERS

In 1961, Minnesota native Edgar Hetteen started a company called Arctic Enterprises. A year later he introduced the red Arctic Cat 100—and the rest is history. Today, Arctic Cat offers dozens of snowmobiles, including the kid-friendly Sno Pro 120.

Brothers Jake (left) and Manny Drexler drive Sno Pro 120 sleds at a race in Mansfield, Wisconsin, in 2009.

Polar Machines

Another of Hetteen's companies, Polaris Industries, grew into a snowmobiling success story. The Polaris Colt and Mustang models were popular in the 1960s. The powerful Indy 500 model, introduced in 1989, remains a legend in the sport.

A Player from Japan

Yamaha burst onto the scene in 1968 with the SL350—a rare collector's item these days. Yamaha was already famous for its motorcycles. Its Phazer line of snowmobiles, launched in 1984, continues to produce top performers.

The Yamaha Phazer was *Snow Goer* magazine's 2007 Snowmobile of the Year.

Blasts from the Past

The International Snowmobile Hall of Fame and Museum in St. Germain, Wisconsin, celebrates the history of snowmobiles and the people who ride them. More than sixty vintage snowmobiles are on display. Other exhibits include trophies, clothing, and photographs of the sport's greatest riders.

SO YOU WANT TO BE A SLED HEAD?

Before you win your first race, you have to learn how to ride a snowmobile. Luckily, it is pretty easy for kids to become sled heads.

An X-treme Sport

Many first-time snowmobilers learn about the sport in the same way. When they are kids, they watch the extreme snowmobile events during ESPN's Winter X Games. Then they ask their parents if they can try out the sport. On a family vacation to a snowy state, they might participate in a program for beginning snowmobilers. Experienced instructors give them lessons on a safe, kid-friendly machine—and they are instantly hooked!

Watch the Pros

Another way to learn about snowmobile racing is to go to a race yourself. Ask your parents to help you look for a professional race in your area. When you get there, soak in as much information as you can. If there are kids at the event, ask them how they started racing. They can give you lots of useful tips. And don't be afraid to talk to the pros. Ask them questions about the sport, the equipment, and the lifestyle. Remember: Every professional snowmobile racer started out as a beginner.

Brett Turcotte (front) and Brett Bender race in the snocross event at the 2007 Winter X Games in Colorado.

SHOPPING FOR SLEDS

Do you want to buy a used or new snowmobile? Here are some useful tips.

Buying a New Snowmobile

- Before you shop, decide how much money you want to spend. New snowmobiles start at a few thousand dollars and can cost as much as $12,000. Don't forget that you'll also need a trailer, accessories, and clothing.

- Research the latest models to find the machine that fits the type of riding or racing you want to do. Consider the engine size, track, suspension, brake and other safety

Kid racer Abbie Kuklinski rides her sled to the finish line at the Eagle River Derby World Championships in 2009.

equipment, comfort, and overall appearance. Check the manufacturers' Web sites, or visit an authorized dealer.

- Try out several different models.

Buying a Used Snowmobile

- Consider the price and type of machine you want. Used sleds are generally cheaper than new ones.

- Ask about used models at your local snowmobile dealer. Also check classified

Mechanical experts can tell you if you're getting a good deal on a used sled.

ads on the Internet and in local newspapers.

- Find a friend or mechanic who is familiar with snowmobiles. Have this person inspect the sled you want to buy.

- Take the sled for a test-drive.

License, Registration, and Safety, Please

Every U.S. state requires that snowmobiles be registered. In some states you need a special driver's license. Many states also have mandatory driving and safety courses for kids. For more details, check your state's official Web site or ask a local snowmobile dealer.

MEET THE MACHINES

There are several different types of snowmobiles. Each type is designed for a particular style of riding and terrain.

Trail Sleds

These snowmobiles have small- to medium-size engines, ranging from 60 to 70 horsepower. Most trail sleds are light, easy to handle, and inexpensive. They are good entry-level machines for beginner snowmobilers.

Performance Sleds

Experienced sled heads go for a performance model. Engines are 120 horsepower and larger—which means the sleds can easily go 80 miles per hour (mph) or faster. Different performance models are built for snocross, oval-shaped tracks, and freestyle racing.

Touring Sleds

Recreational snowmobilers ride long distances on these powerful, comfortable sleds. Heated seats fit two riders, and longer tracks provide a smooth ride.

Mountain Sleds

High-horsepower engines and long tracks get these sleds up steep mountains and through deep snow. Racers use special mountain sleds in hillclimb events.

Utility Sleds

Farmers, ranchers, loggers, ski patrollers, and other outdoor workers use utility sleds during snowy months. They are built to get the job done.

BODY BASICS

Here are the basic parts of a snowmobile.

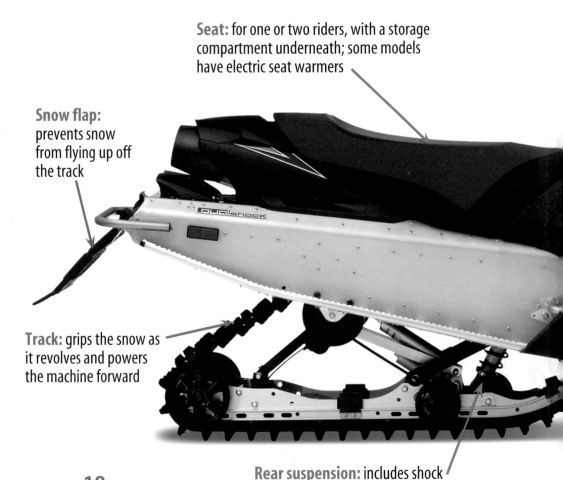

Seat: for one or two riders, with a storage compartment underneath; some models have electric seat warmers

Snow flap: prevents snow from flying up off the track

Track: grips the snow as it revolves and powers the machine forward

Rear suspension: includes shock absorbers for a smooth ride

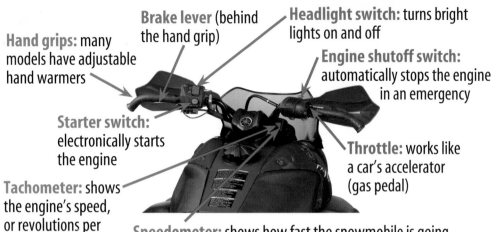

Brake lever (behind the hand grip)

Headlight switch: turns bright lights on and off

Hand grips: many models have adjustable hand warmers

Engine shutoff switch: automatically stops the engine in an emergency

Starter switch: electronically starts the engine

Throttle: works like a car's accelerator (gas pedal)

Tachometer: shows the engine's speed, or revolutions per minute (rpm)

Speedometer: shows how fast the snowmobile is going

Other gauges: additional gauges show gas level, oil temperature, miles traveled, and other measurements

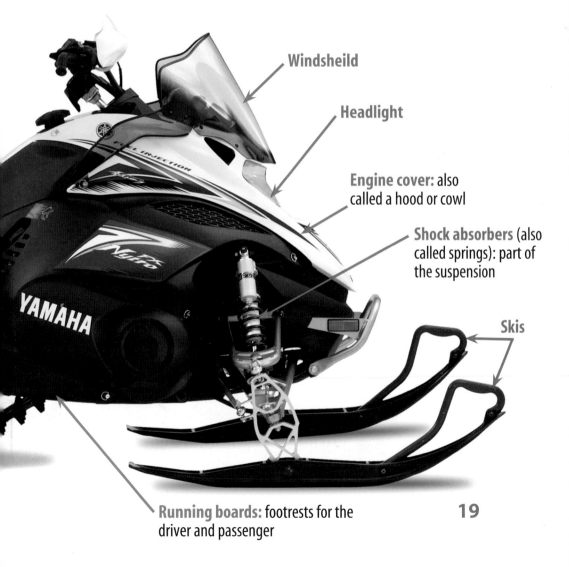

Windsheild

Headlight

Engine cover: also called a hood or cowl

Shock absorbers (also called springs): part of the suspension

Skis

Running boards: footrests for the driver and passenger

19

Shown here is the two-stroke engine of a 2003 Ski-Doo.

UNDER THE HOOD

Ever since snowmobiles were invented, people have complained that the engines are too noisy and create too much air pollution. Sled manufacturers have worked hard to correct these problems.

Two-Stroke Engines

Until recently, snowmobiles were powered by two-stroke engines. These engines are light, powerful, and inexpensive. Old two-stroke engines can be messy, though, because you have to mix oil with gas. This mixture results in dirty exhaust. Two-stroke engines used to be very loud. However, engineers have developed two-stroke engines that don't use an oil-gas mixture and are quieter.

Four-Stroke Engines

Until recently, many snowmobile manufacturers were switching to four-stroke engines. These engines have more moving parts. They are heavier and less powerful than two-stroke engines, but they can be cleaner and less noisy. Sled makers have improved four-stroke engines, so now they can compete with two-stroke engines.

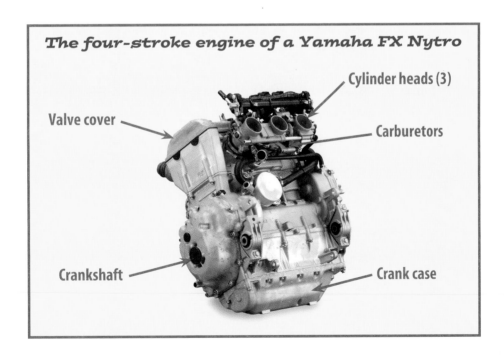

The four-stroke engine of a Yamaha FX Nytro

Cylinder heads (3)

Valve cover

Carburetors

Crankshaft

Crank case

10

An official checks a snowmobile's track to make sure it follows the racing rules.

FOLLOW THE TRACKS

Snowmobiles move on revolving tracks that look like they have teeth. They are similar to the tracks on bulldozers and army tanks.

Teeth of Rubber

Snowmobile tracks used to be made of flexible but tough rubber. Many of today's models have tracks made of Kevlar and other strong, man-made materials. The track is actually a series of hard strips linked together. Each strip is lined with "teeth" that grip snow and ice. Like cleats on athletic shoes or treads on bicycle tires, the teeth provide traction and prevent slipping.

Grips on the Move

The track revolves on a series of wheels and a drive belt. Tracks are between 10 and 15 inches wide. Wider tracks are used on heavier snowmobiles designed for zooming up mountainsides.

Goin' Where There's No Snowin'

Snowmobile tracks can grip more than just snow and ice. They dig in to asphalt and grass, too! Sled heads hold drag races on these unfrozen surfaces. Grass drags are especially popular at the annual Hay Days, a snowmobile festival held every September in Forest Lake, Minnesota.

Snowmobilers trade white snow for green grass at a drag in Wausau, Wisconsin.

SLED SAFETY

All snowmobilers should think of safety first. Snowmobiles are heavy, powerful motor vehicles that can reach high speeds. Drivers are responsible for their own safety, as well as the safety of their passengers, fellow riders, pedestrians, and even wildlife.

Safe Technology
Manufacturers add lots of safety features to their sleds. These features include disc brakes,

Snowmobilers share the "road" with a bison at Yellowstone National Park in Wyoming.

engine "kill" switches, lights, and reflectors. Many snowmobile dealers offer driver training and safety classes.

Club Rules

Snowmobile clubs expect their members to obey local riding laws, to stay on marked trails, and to respect the environment. Mountain riders have to be especially careful to avoid avalanches. The International Snowmobile Manufacturers Association has created a program called Safe Riders: You Make Snowmobiling Safe. (See Further Reading for more information.)

Handy Safety Signals

Safe snowmobilers use these basic hand signals:

 Left turn: left arm extended straight out

 Right turn: left arm out, forearm raised, with elbow at a 90-degree angle

 Stop: left arm raised straight up with palm of hand flat

 Slow: left arm out and angled toward the ground

 Sleds following: arm raised, elbow bent with thumb pointing backward, arm moving forward and backward over shoulder

 Last sled in line: Left arm raised at shoulder height, elbow bent, and forearm vertical with hand in a fist

Safely dressed racers check out the track before their event. Popular gear brands include FXR, Arctiva, and Coldwave.

LOOKING GOOD, STAYING WARM

Riding on a snowmobile is a thrilling experience. It's a chilling one, too, so be sure to bundle up. Layering is the key. Start with long underwear and warm socks. Then add a turtleneck shirt, a sweater, comfortable pants, waterproof snow pants, and a jacket. The final layer includes a hat, gloves, and thick, insulated boots.

A Padded Ride

Dress for safety, whether you're riding for pleasure or competing in a race. Protective gear will keep you safe in case of a fall or crash. Always wear an approved helmet with a face guard and eye protection. Racers are required to wear clothing, gloves, and boots with extra padding and guards.

Champion kid racer Mason Raffauf stays safe with style!

Safe Sledding Checklist

Make sure you have all these items before you head to the trail:

- ✔ helmet
- ✔ eye protection (goggles, glasses)
- ✔ face guard
- ✔ reinforced pants and jacket
- ✔ high-top boots
- ✔ padded gloves
- ✔ first-aid kit
- ✔ tool kit
- ✔ pocketknife
- ✔ rope
- ✔ compass, map, or GPS device
- ✔ energy bars
- ✔ flashlight, flares
- ✔ sunscreen
- ✔ cell phone

RIDER BEWARE!

Snowmobilers need to operate their sleds safely— especially when they're racing. In this risky sport, preventing accidents is a top priority.

Hazards for Racers

Snocross racers speed around a twisting course filled with jumps and other obstacles. It's easy to imagine the sleds bumping into each other, and they often do. Freestylers doing mid-air flips and other aerobatic maneuvers can wipe out—or "biff," as sled heads like to say. Before you even think about entering a

Just like cars on a road, snowmobiles stay in single file on the trail.

snowmobile race, learn how to operate a sled in *all* types of conditions.

On the Trail

When riding with family and friends for fun, always follow the rules of the "road." On trails, ride in single file. Keep a safe distance between sleds. Riding on frozen ponds, lakes, and rivers can be fun, but be sure the ice is thick and completely frozen. Mountain riders must always be aware of avalanche conditions when riding through fresh snow.

Read Between the Signs

Snowmobilers riding on snow-packed roads must obey local traffic laws, including stop, yield, one-way, and speed limit signs. There are various signs on snowmobile trails, too. Pay special attention to signs marking designated trails. Snowmobilers should always stay off private property.

FOLLOW ROAD TO TRAIL

READY...SET...GO!

Early snowmobile racing was pretty simple—line up side by side, start driving, and see who crosses the finish line first. Today there are several types of snowmobile races.

Ice Ovals This is one of the original types of snowmobile racing. As in NASCAR, competitors zoom around an oval track—but this one is made of ice or hard-packed snow.

Hillclimb One at a time, racers blast up a steep mountainside course filled with gates, deep ruts, and other obstacles. The fastest time wins.

Snowmobilers race to the finish at a twenty-lap ice oval event at the World Championship Snowmobile Derby.

Hillcross racers take a big jump on a tough uphill track. Sled heads as young as six compete in hillcross.

Hillcross Groups of riders race up a ski-hill course featuring moguls, "washboard" bumps, and other jumps at speeds over 70 mph. The first racer to the top wins.

Drags In a drag race, the idea is to line up and go as fast as you can. These events are run on straight courses set up on snow, grass, and asphalt.

Cross-country Cross-country competitors race on a long course through fields, forests, lakes, and other frozen terrain.

Mechanical Mushing

Mushers command dogsled teams that race over long, snowy distances. Snowmobilers now compete in similar races—minus the dogs. The most famous is the Iron Dog, the longest cross-country snowmobile race in the world. It covers nearly 2,000 miles, from Wasilla to Nome to Fairbanks, Alaska.

X GAMES MARK THE SPOT

The most extreme snowmobile racing happens at the annual Winter X Games. Gold, silver, and bronze medals are awarded in every event.

Snocross

This is the most popular kind of snowmobile racing. Groups of racers speed along a difficult course filled with jumps, bumps, and sharp turns. They reach speeds of over 60 mph and get "big air" off jumps, flying as high as 30 feet.

The Best Racers

The Winter X Games, televised in either January or February on ESPN2, showcase the world's thirty-two best snocross racers. In the first round, groups of eight race in four heats (phases). The top twenty-four racers move on to the second round, which features two heats of twelve competitors. Twelve of these racers advance to the final, which consists of one 20-lap race.

Hats Off to Wisconsin

Every winter since 1964, Eagle River, Wisconsin, has hosted the World Championship Snowmobile Derby. The weekend-long event features snocross and ice oval races for professionals, semi-pros, amateurs, teens, and kids. Racers compete for more than $130,000 in cash, prizes, and trophies. The derby attracts more than 1,400 racers and 30,000 spectators.

Kevin Kuklinski leads in the eight- to twelve-year old race at Eagle River in 2009.

SLED HEADS VS. GRAVITY

Snowmobiles were not originally designed to fly through the air—but don't tell that to the daredevils who compete in freestyle races. Judges grade freestylers on difficulty, style, and success in "sticking" all sorts of mid-air tricks.

Jumps and Flips

It's truly amazing to watch these fearless men and women twist and turn themselves and their hulking machines 20 or 30 feet off the ground.

A member of a freestyle group called the Slednecks wows the crowd with a trick.

They buzz around a series of curved jumps. Rider and sled catapult high and far into the frosty air. They defy gravity, sometimes even doing complete 360-degree flips.

Speed & Style

The third and final Winter X Games snowmobile event is called Speed & Style. It combines the quickness of snocross and the skill of freestyle into one event. Eight riders compete in head-to-head heats.

Wet and Wild

During the summer, some snowmobilers just can't wait until the snow returns to get back on their sleds. Watercross is the extreme sport for them. They take off from the shore on light, high-speed snowmobiles. The challenge is to keep the track spinning fast enough to whip the sled across the water—and to avoid sinking. Watercross competitions include drags and oval races.

Joe Parsons soars into the air at the Winter X Games freestyle event in January 2009. Parsons won the gold medal.

STAR RIDERS

Some older snowmobile racers have been riding for a long time, but lots of young sled heads are joining them. Here are some of the hottest names in snowmobile racing.

Joe Parsons

"I got into snowmobiling as a kid and started racing when I was twelve," says Joe Parsons of Yakima, Washington. Parsons raced snocross before switching to freestyle in 2007. He got the hang of the new sport pretty quickly. At the 2009 Winter X Games, Parsons took home gold medals in the freestyle and Speed & Style events.

Kylie Abrahamson

Kylie's dad and older brother introduced her to snocross when she was ten. Over the next decade, Kylie became one of the sport's top female racers. In 2008, she won the Pro Women Championship and was named Pro Women Racer of the Year. What's her secret to success? "I have to wear my Under Armour shirt and checkered-flag socks in every race," Abrahamson says.

Kid Racer Spotlight: James Johnstad

Sixteen-year-old James Johnstad has been riding with his family for most of his life. He started snocross racing when he was ten and has been successful ever since. Competing in junior class events for the Avalanche Team, Johnstad won ten national races in 2008. In 2009, he won the ISOC Junior National Championships in two different age classes. "James is a determined racer who always shows great talent and sportsmanship," says Avalanche Team owner Mike Glefke. Watch for Johnstad's name in the Winter X Games before too long!

SLICK MY SLED

When brand-new snowmobiles leave the factory, they are considered stock models. Each one is exactly the same, with all its original parts. But sled heads love to buy new snowmobiles and then add and subtract parts.

This Yamaha RX-1 was custom-built to climb mountains in up to 3 feet of powdery snow. It has a 330-horsepower engine and weighs 535 pounds.

At the Dealer

Snowmobile dealers sell a variety of custom exhaust systems, snow flaps, mirrors, and seats. Creative paints jobs are popular, too.

Minor Changes

Some snowmobile racing events only allow stock machines. All competitors must race the same type of sleds, so no one has an unfair advantage. In other events, like freestyle, racers are allowed to customize their engines, exhausts, skis, shocks, handlebars, and other parts.

Sled makers used special materials to make this snowmobile as light as possible. It weighs in at 445 pounds.

Custom Tricks

The editors at *SnoWest*, a magazine for snowmobilers, customized a 2009 Yamaha Nytro MTX. With the help of a creative team at Timbersled Products, a shop for making custom sleds, they took a stock Nytro and turned it into one mean machine.

A Yamaha Nytro MTX

THE FAMILY THAT SLEDS TOGETHER . . .

Now you're an experienced snowmobile racer, and you're off to another race. You have made it to the final. On the last lap, you slip past the leader and take the checkered flag. Your family applauds as you receive your trophy.

After the Race

The fun is not over yet, though. This race was sponsored by a local snowmobile club. The club has invited the racers and their families to hang around for some fun riding on miles of trails near the snocross course.

An Afternoon in the Snow

Your dad has brought his own machine to the event. Your mom and sister are ready to try snowmobiling for the first time. Your sister rents a Sno Pro 120; your mom chooses a 600cc trail model. After a driving lesson, you join a group of club members for an afternoon ride.

Join the Club!

One of the best ways for families to get into the sport is to join a club. If you're interested, ask a local snowmobile dealer about clubs in your area.

In this snowmobile club's parking lot, there are more sleds than cars!

20

Vendors at Hay Days get serious about machines.

HAPPY HAY DAYS

Every summer, sled heads start getting itchy. Winter is still a ways off, but they can hardly wait to get back in their sleds. Thank goodness for Hay Days.

Hay Days is a snowmobile extravaganza, held every year on the first weekend after Labor Day in Forest Lake, Minnesota. Organizers claim it is the world's largest snowmobile event.

In on the Action

These days, Hay Days attracts about 30,000 people. The big four sled manufacturers— Arctic Cat, Polaris, Ski-Doo, and Yamaha— are there to show off their new sleds. There are also dozens of companies that make snowmobile clothing, gear, and custom parts. People can buy and sell used snowmobile gear in a giant swap meet.

Extreme freestyle rider Jimmy Blaze greets fans after doing a backflip on his sled at Hay Days.

Winter Sports in Summer

Sled heads look forward to the grass drag races and freestyle riding events at Hay Days. It's a warm-weather warm-up for another season of snowmobiling.

Get Your Game On

Thanks to video games, you can test your snowmobiling skills even if there's no snow outside. Get a feel for snocross in the PlayStation 2 game featuring the legendary racer Blair Morgan. *Kawasaki Snowmobiles*, created for the Wii system, lets players fly over bumps and jumps.

GLOSSARY

aerobatic—Describing spectacular stunts, such as flips and twists, that are performed in the air.

avalanches—Large amounts of snow and ice falling down a mountainside.

catapult—To fling an object into the air.

cubic centimeters—Metric measurements used to describe an engine's size, abbreviated as cc.

cylinder—The cylindrical (rounded) part of an engine in which a piston moves up and down to generate power.

disc brakes—A brake system in which pads squeeze a rotating cylinder to slow and stop a vehicle.

exhaust—Fumes that come from an engine's exhaust pipe.

extravaganza—A big show or event.

gauge—A tool or instrument used to measure something.

groomed—Packed down and smoothed, usually by a special machine.

horsepower—A unit of power equal to 746 watts; abbreviated as hp.

insulated—Protected from extreme cold or heat.

manufacturers—People or companies that make products.

recreational—Used for pleasure rather than work.

revolves—Moves in the shape of a circle or oval.

suspension—A system of springs and shock absorbers that reduce impact of bumps and uneven surfaces for drivers and passengers of vehicles.

terrain—The characteristics of an area of land, such as rocky, wet, or sandy.

traction—The ability to grip a surface.

FURTHER READING

Books

Aksomitis, Linda and David. *Illustrated Guide to Snowmobile Racing.* Hudson, Wis.: Iconografix, 2006.

Budd, E. S. *Snowmobiles.* Chanhassen, Minn.: Child's World, 2004.

Marx, Mandy R. *Extreme Snowmobiling.* Mankato, Minn.: Capstone Press, 2006.

Salas, Laura Purdie. *Snowmobiling.* Mankato, Minn.: Capstone Press, 2008.

Web Sites

International Series of Champions—*the official site of ISOC, an organization that promotes snocross races across the United States and Canada*
<www.isocracing.com>

International Snowmobile Manufacturers Association—*find information about the four major snowmobile manufacturers: Arctic Cat, Ski-Doo, Polaris, and Yamaha*
<www.snowmobile.org>

ESPN's Winter X Games—*learn about all the extreme sports, events, and athletes featured at the Winter X Games*
<www.espn.go.com/action/xgames/index>

INDEX

A

Abrahamson, Kylie, 37
Arctic Cat, 10

B

Bender, Brett, 12
Blaze, Jimmy, 43
Bombardier, Joseph-Armand, 9
buying snowmobiles, 13, 14–15

C

clothing, 26–27
clubs, 6, 25, 41
cross-country racing, 31
customizing snowmobiles, 38–39

D

drag racing, 7, 23, 31, 35
Drexler, Jake and Manny, 10

E

engines, 20–21

F

freestyle racing, 17, 28, 34–37, 39

H

Hay Days, 23, 42–43
Hetteen, Edgar, 10
hillclimbing, 17, 30–31
history, 8–11

I

ice, riding on, 6, 16, 29, 30, 33
International Snowmobile Hall of
    Fame and Museum, 11
Iron Dog race, 31

J

Johnstad, James, 37
jumping, 12, 31, 32, 33, 34–35, 36

K

Kégresse, Adolphe, 9
Kuklinski, Abbie, 14
Kuklinski, Kevin, 33

L

learning to ride, 12–13, 29

M

mountain riding, 17, 23, 25, 29, 38

O

oval racing, 16, 17, 30, 33, 35

P

Parsons, Joe, 36–37
performance sleds, 17
Polaris Industries, 10–11

R

racing, 6–7, 28–37, 39, 40
Raffauf, Mason, 27

S

safety, 15, 24–25, 27, 28–29
Ski-Doos, 9, 20
snocross racing, 6–7, 12, 17, 28, 32–33,
    35, 36, 37, 40
snowmobiles
    parts of, 18–23
    types of, 16–17
Speed & Style racing, 35, 37
states
    snowiest, 5
    snowmobile registration, 7

T

touring sleds, 17
tracks, 22–23
trails, 6, 28, 29
trail sleds, 16–17
Turcotte, Brett, 12

U

utility sleds, 17

V

video games, 43

W

watercross racing, 35
Winter X Games, 12, 13, 32–33, 35, 36,
    37
World Championship Snowmobile
    Derby, 14, 30, 33

Y

Yamaha, 11, 21, 38, 39